Original title:
Diving into the Current

Copyright © 2025 Creative Arts Management OÜ
All rights reserved.

Author: Rory Fitzgerald
ISBN HARDBACK: 978-1-80587-431-7
ISBN PAPERBACK: 978-1-80587-901-5

The Water's Embrace

In a splash, the fish declare,
"What's up? We've got room to share!"
Bubbles giggle, water sways,
Kicking fins in silly ways.

Frogs wear goggles, what a sight,
Synchronized, they leap with might.
The turtles waddle with such grace,
Waving hi, it's a splashy race.

Flowing Parallels

Streams of silver twist and twine,
Fishy friends sip sparkling brine.
An otter chills, with snacky cheer,
"Want some algae? It's quite dear!"

Thoughts like bubbles float away,
Zany dreams, come out to play.
Currents twist in joyful glee,
In this whirlpool, just be free!

Secrets of the Deep

Octopi in bowties dance,
Throwing parties, what a chance!
Anemones play peekaboo,
"Did you see? I just left you!"

Crabs in suits negotiate,
"Let's trade shells—don't be late!"
Secrets murmur through the waves,
Giggles in the deep sea caves.

The Cascade of Moments

Waterfalls that laugh and sing,
Bouncing off the rocks, they fling.
"Catch me now!" they gleefully shout,
As splashes echo, laughter's route.

Rafts of ducks, a quacky crew,
Paddling fast, their rascals brew.
Moments cascade, a joyful race,
In this river, find your place.

Beneath the Surface

Bubbles rise, fish smile wide,
A crab gives a thumbs-up, not one to hide.
Seaweed giggles, swaying low,
Octopuses spin in a disco show.

A turtle on roller skates zooms by,
Splashing water as he starts to fly.
Jellyfish waltz with a twist and a twirl,
Under the sea, chaos begins to swirl.

Tides of Transformation

A starfish puts on a fancy hat,
Pretending to be a cool acrobat.
Waves bring in gossip from the shore,
Where seagulls squawk of ocean lore.

A treasure chest full of rubber ducks,
Mermaids laugh, there's no need for luck.
Fish in sunglasses, looking so fly,
They swim through the sea, as time passes by.

The Ripple Effect

An otter slides down a slippery rock,
With a cannonball, he sends a big shock.
The splash reaches a clam who shouts, "Hey!
Don't drown my pearls, I need them for play!"

Crabs play tag, dodging all the fuss,
They wiggle and squirm, adding to the rush.
Each little wave brings a brand new game,
In this wacky sea, nothing is the same.

Uncharted Waters

On a treasure map, there's an 'X' so bright,
But it leads to a party of pure delight.
Sardines serve drinks, and plankton dance,
Under the sea, they all take a chance.

A dolphin does flips, while a whale sings songs,
In this underwater world, nobody's wrong.
With laughter and bubbles creating a cheer,
Every splash brings joy, that much is clear.

The Dance of the Sea

The ocean sways with a playful grin,
Fish in tuxedos spin and spin.
A crab in a hat, what a peculiar sight,
Doing the cha-cha 'til the morning light.

Waves drop beats, as seagulls croon,
The starfish jams, under the moon.
A dolphin flips with a splash of glee,
Who knew the ocean was so dance-y?

A Stream of Dreams

In a babbling brook, the frogs all sing,
Wearing their crowns, they're just the thing.
A turtle in shades paddles by with style,
While fish throw a party, oh such a pile!

Driftwood floats by with a silly grin,
Holding on tightly to a grin within.
A beaver's beat with a drum made of bark,
Creating a rhythm from dawn until dark.

In the Heart of the Current

The river flows with a cheeky swirl,
Where otters play hopscotch, give it a twirl.
Eels buzzing tunes with a funky flare,
While turtles giggle, floating without a care.

Bubbles rise, little voices shout,
With a splash of laughter, there's no doubt.
The fish throw confetti, what a brave feat,
Making the banks their fun little seat.

Fluid Wanderings

Winding paths of the waterway's twist,
A frog on a lily, oh how he can't resist.
He leaps for a dance; oops! Down he goes,
A splash and a splash, in the water he shows!

A snail in a shell, with a hat on the side,
Says, "Join me, dear fish, for a lazy joyride!"
Jellyfish join in with their wobbly jig,
Making light of life, each groove is so big!

Whispers of the Tide

Bubbles rise like giggles, oh what a sight,
With fins that flutter, I swim with delight.
A dance with the fishes, in seaweed I hide,
Round and round they twirl, let's take a wild ride!

Splashing and flapping, I chase after rays,
The sea's a wild dance floor, with waves in a craze.
A jellyfish wobbles, I can't help but laugh,
While crabs do the cha-cha, in our underwater half.

Currents of Change

The water's a joker, it pulls and it tugs,
I swim like a noodle, receiving its hugs.
Sea cucumbers chuckle, I wobble and sway,
A fish swirls around, saying, 'Come on, let's play!'

With every sharp turn, oh the giggles abound,
A whirlpool of laughter, where silliness is found.
An octopus winks, pulls a prank with its ink,
While I whirl in delight, giving critics a think.

The Depths Await

Down in the deep, where the silly things roam,
I ride on a sea slug, it's almost like foam.
With each bumbling splash, my laughter flows free,
A clownfish appears, saying, 'Join the big spree!'

In kelp forests green, we spin in a ring,
The seahorses giggle, as I start to sing.
With bubbles as beats, we dance through the night,
In this underwater ball, we twirl with delight!

Tides of Transformation

A wave crashes in, with a splat and a cheer,
I'm transformed to a dolphin, let's spread some good cheer!
With jumps and with flips, I show off my flair,
While a turtle rolls by, too slow for the dare.

The tide's a comedian, it teases my tail,
I chase after sea urchins, through laughter I sail.
With clams that keep chuckling, and fish that just grin,
I flip and I flop, letting the fun begin!

The Calm Before the Surge

The sea is a pillow, soft and wide,
Where fish wear their goggles, and crabs take a ride.
A seagull lands singing, a merry old tune,
While a starfish groans, 'Is it too soon?'

The beach ball is bouncing, off into the waves,
While jellyfish giggle, all dressed up like knaves.
The tide whispers humor, jokes made of foam,
And the sandcastles wobble, longing for home.

Spirals in the Sand

Footprints leading nowhere, a spiraled path,
Where the sand wants to tickle, and dolphins just laugh.
Seashells tell stories, in their shell-like debates,
While crabs host a dance where everyone waits.

A jellyfish juggles, it's quite a grand show,
While octopuses play hide and seek in a row.
And the sun wears a grin, as it gets brighter still,
As laughter breaks out on the dune-topped hill.

Moving with the Waters

The current is a dancer, twirling with glee,
As flip-flops get carried, like ships on the sea.
Turtles in tuxedos swim past with a cheer,
While fish tell cold jokes that only they hear.

A wave gives a nod, as surfers take flight,
With more crashes than grace, oh, what a sight!
Splashing and laughing, it's all in good fun,
As the ocean keeps smiling, in the warmth of the sun.

The Ocean's Secrets

What lies beneath? A mystery we face,
With mermaids and pirates, in a magical place.
Whales whisper secrets, they're very well known,
While sea cucumbers lounge, and make it their own.

Coral reefs giggle, in colors so bright,
As turtles remind us to take it light.
And while clams keep their pearls hidden deep in their shells,
The ocean grins broadly, with all of its spells.

Ripples of the Soul

When splashes happen, who can tell?
A fishy tale, or it's just a spell.
The bubbles dance, a silly show,
While salty grins begin to grow.

A splash from me, a wave from you,
A rubber duck floats in the queue.
We laugh and tipple, joy's the goal,
Making ripples from the soul.

The seagulls squawk with cheeky flair,
As waves toss seaweed through the air.
We trade our secrets with a pout,
But giggles turn our frowns about.

The ocean's laughter, a grand display,
As we join in the frolic play.
In every splash, something droll,
In these ripples, we find our roll.

Secrets in the Blue

Underneath the water, what do we find?
A sock and a boat, oh never mind!
A mermaid's giggle, a turtle's wink,
All the secrets make us think.

The ocean holds a fashion show,
With jellyfish gowns stealing the glow.
Crabs strut by, with pinching pride,
In this deep blue, jokes can't hide.

A treasure chest? Just an old shoe,
But with a sparkle, it seems brand new.
Lost sunglasses turn to sunlit stars,
In this blue world, we're all bizarre.

Whispers up high, and splashes down low,
Each wave sings tunes we all know.
In the laughter and the hues,
We share the secrets of the blue.

Driftwood Dreams

Floating by, oh what do we see?
A log that dreams of being a tree.
Driftwood tales of faraway lands,
With shells and sand in whimsical strands.

The barnacle's gossip, sticky and thick,
Creating jokes with a salty flick.
In the surf, we chase our schemes,
Laughing hard at driftwood dreams.

Each piece carries a story, a tale,
Of distant shores and ocean trails.
The seaweed wiggles, a comical scene,
In our floating world, we're all a mean.

With a wink from a wave, we make our drive,
In this woodsy dance, we feel alive.
Our laughter echoing through the beams,
Sailing through our driftwood dreams.

Below the Glittering Surface

Beneath the sparkles, what do you see?
A fish on a skateboard, whoa, let it be!
The playful bubbles giggle loud,
As we cannonball, feeling proud.

Coral castles hold a grand debate,
With sea cucumbers deciding fate.
An octopus wearing a royal crown,
Mumbling wise words upside down.

The seabed parties in shades of bright,
Starfish dance and twirl in delight.
With conch shells shouting jokes and cheers,
The tide swells up our giggling gears.

In the sparkling depths, we make a mess,
Sharing laughter, surely we're blessed.
For below the surface, joy will traverse,
Dancing freely in this curious universe.

The Soul's Tsunami

Splashing about with grace,
A fish takes my place,
With fins all a-glimmer,
I swim like a winner.

Caught in a whirlpool's hug,
I wiggle and tug,
I just wanted to float,
Where's my life boat?

The jellyfish tides tease,
They jive with such ease,
I try to escape, beg,
But they dance on my leg.

With bubbles of laughter rise,
A flock of bright fries,
Who knew fish could be jesters,
Performing grand gestures?

The Call of the Deep

Underwater, oh what a sight,
A sea cucumber's quite polite,
It waves with a bubbly cheer,
While I ponder my next beer.

The octopus shows off its flair,
A blurry dance, quite rare,
I trip over a coral rock,
This is no fun, just a mock!

The dolphins take a bow,
They laugh, oh wow!
I flip and flop like a fool,
In this slippery pool.

But all in this blue, I grin,
This madness is my kin,
With gills and fins, I'll thrive,
Splashing in this funny dive!

Currents We Cannot See

Riding waves, I float on by,
A crab waves hello, oh my!
It pinches my toe in jest,
Now that's a true underwater fest!

The seaweed giggles and sways,
In this wild, wacky maze,
I tried to dance with a shark,
But it swam off into the dark.

Unseen currents pull and tease,
Each pull's like a tickling breeze,
I may not be a dolphin ace,
But I sure have won the race!

With every splash, a silly grin,
Finding joy where I begin,
This playful plunge, oh what bliss,
Who knew the sea could be this?

A Cascade of Thoughts

In rippling thoughts, I float away,
Like a fish gone astray,
With bubbles of wild ideas,
And giggles that last for years.

Sharks wear glasses? It's absurd!
A voice whispers, 'Have you heard?'
In the coral, dreams collide,
A fish parade, join the ride!

The starfish plays tag with a grouper,
While I'm here just being a trooper,
I lost my snack, now I pout,
But there's laughter all about.

Who knew the deep could be so fun?
Splashing joy is never done,
In this silly underwater dance,
Every wave gives life a chance!

In the Flow of Time

Splashing waves, we dance with glee,
Fishy faces tease the sea.
Time slips by like slippery eels,
Giggles echo, joy reveals.

Floating through the playful tide,
Comical cycles, we can't hide.
Ticklish crabs pinch, what a sight,
We're the jesters, full of light.

Riding bubbles, we take flight,
Finding laughter, pure delight.
In this whirlpool, fun's on cue,
Time doesn't matter, just me and you.

The Beauty of Drift

Gliding smoothly, we lose our way,
Floating cups and frisbees play.
A sea of plastic, whoops! A boat,
Fish are laughing, quite a quote.

Drifting past, a turtle grins,
It's a party where fun begins.
Time to tumble, slip, and slide,
With ocean waves, we take a ride.

Seaweed wigs and coral crowns,
In this current, nobody frowns.
Giggles bubble, fish parade,
In this drift, good times are made.

Journey Through the Blue

We're off on a whimsical quest,
Flippers flapping, we're the best!
Who knew whales could crack a smile?
Every corner has fun in style.

Bubbles pop, a jellyfish jive,
Octopuses doin' high-five.
Sea turtles sweep and swirl around,
In this dance, joy's always found.

Fish sing songs with silly tunes,
The ocean floor, our fun commune.
Splashing laughter fills the air,
Through the blue without a care.

The Ocean's Pulse

Ping-pong rhythms of the tide,
Dancing crabs take us for a ride.
With each wave, a chuckle flows,
Who would guess how much fun it grows?

Waves do the twist, a funny spin,
Sharks in bowties swim and grin.
Mermaids giggle as they flit,
Painting seashells, bit by bit.

Seashells play drums, we join the beat,
With jellybeans, a tasty treat.
In this pulse, we find our glee,
Living life so blissfully free.

The Art of Immersion

Plunge in quick, with belly flop,
Water splashes, hear the plop.
Fish now stare with bulging eyes,
As I swim by with frantic sighs.

Fins and flippers, what a sight,
Gentle waves, oh what a flight.
Goggles fogged and my hair's a mess,
Mermaid dreams turned into stress.

Fishy friends in the murky blue,
Ask me, friend, do you need a clue?
A flip, a splash, I lose my grace,
Water's fun, but I'm off pace!

Wet and wild, I laugh so loud,
Making bubbles, feeling proud.
Though I may finish out of breath,
I'll jump right back, ignore the depth.

The Calm Within Chaos

Waves crash down in a comical style,
A surfboard flips, with a flailing smile.
Underneath the foam, I'm a clown,
Riding tides while I almost drown.

Seagulls squawk, like they know the score,
I tumble and giggle, then roll on the shore.
Driftwood dances, dodging my feet,
Be careful, they say! You're in for a treat.

The ocean grins, it sways and spins,
I come to play, where chaos begins.
With water wings, I float like a feather,
No one warned me to check the weather!

Laughter echoes, a whimsical tune,
As I chase jellyfish, under the moon.
In this chaos, joy finds a way,
Come join the fun, let's splash and play!

A Tryst with the Deep

A secret pact with the blues below,
In tangled seaweed, I start to go.
Fishy whispers and bubbles laugh,
As I try to swim, they take a gaffe.

Swirling down with a playful twist,
Caught off guard, can't resist the mist.
Tangled up in my own grand scheme,
Who knew the ocean would burst my dream?

A lonely crab gives me a glare,
While I fumble, splashing everywhere.
I wave goodbye but can't make a run,
In this grand ballet, I'm not the one.

Down I dive, but not with grace,
Just a big splash, and a silly face.
Embracing the chaos, my heart will leap,
In this odd romance, with the deep I keep.

Under the Weight of Water

Giant waves, feel the pressure swell,
I thud like a whale, but oh well!
Underneath, the fish are primed,
For a comedy act, perfectly timed.

Bubble-blowing, is this even fun?
Got lost in the depths, but I'm not done.
With each flop, it's a glorious dance,
Flippers fly, will I get a chance?

But then a grumpy octopus frowns,
As I slip and slide, beneath the crowns.
He rolls his eyes, quite unimpressed,
I'm just trying to enjoy my quest!

With a belly laugh, I take a bow,
Water's my stage, and I'll show you how.
Under the weight, a giggle takes flight,
In these depths, all feels so right.

Voyage into the Abyss

With a splish and a splash, I take the plunge,
My belly flops sound like a thunderous lunge.
Bubbles rise up, tickling my toes,
I giggle and wiggle; where the riptide flows.

Octopuses wave with a curious flair,
Fish give me looks, do they really care?
In a seaweed wig, I dance with glee,
A mermaid spellbound, or just a fishy flea?

My snorkel is leaking, my fins a bit tight,
I swear I'm a dolphin, but swim like a kite.
Every stroke makes a splash, a cartoonish sound,
I'm a clumsy sea creature, in laughter I'm drowned.

So here in the depths, I float with a grin,
In this aquatic rave, where none can chagrin.
The abyss holds treasures, but now I just see,
That laughing's the treasure, the best catch for me.

The Abyss Beckons

The ocean calls with a wink and a wave,
It teases the brave, who don't need to behave.
I zip up my wetsuit, prepare for the dive,
What's waiting below? A tale to contrive!

A turtle shoots past as I twirl like a top,
Doing backflips and splashes, oh, dare I stop?
The jellyfish jiggle right over my head,
I'm a floaty, blobby, aquatic thread!

A shark swims by, with a grin on his face,
I give him a nod; he's got style and grace.
"Just passing through!" he says with a wink,
I burst out in laughter—what do sharks think?

As bubbles escape, like secrets from me,
This show's full of surprises beneath the sea.
The abyss is a party, come join in my fun,
Where even the fish know how to run!

Currents of Reflection

I float on my back, like a shipwrecked queen,
The sun's tickling cheeks, you know what I mean?
My thoughts drift like driftwood, oh, what a sight,
In this bobbing boat of whimsical light.

I see crabs line dancing to the ocean's beat,
While seagulls throw shade from their high-up seat.
A school of fish starts a conga so bright,
In the currents of laughter, we dance day and night.

As sea anemones wave their stylish threads,
I ponder the meaning of jiggly beds.
"Do fish wear pajamas?" I ask in a bind,
The deep whispers back, "Just stay light and kind!"

With salty ambitions and giggles galore,
I float with the waves, who could ask for more?
In bubbly reflections, I shed all my cares,
In this frothy adventure, joy's all that I wear.

Surfing the Veil of Time

On my board, I glide through the shimmering spray,
Each wave a reminder of the silly play.
Surfing through moments, both fast and slow,
The ride's like a rollercoaster, whoa, let's go!

With a tumble and roll, I wipe out with flair,
My friends burst with laughter; they just can't compare.
The ocean's a trickster, keeps throwing me back,
But what's a few splashes on this fun-loving track?

Time drifts like seaweed, swirling in tide,
Every gnarly crash, a joyful slide.
The horizon winks back, with each rolling swell,
The dance of the waves casts a magical spell.

So here on the surface, I surf and I smile,
Each wipeout a moment, I take for a while.
With laughter as my anchor, I'm forever afloat,
In the waves of the future, on happiness's boat!

Surreal Streams

In a water park, we laughed out loud,
Fighting waves, feeling quite proud.
Rubber duckies drifting by,
Swirling around, oh me, oh my!

Flipping flops and funny dives,
Chasing fish with silly vibes.
Splashing friends with giggling glee,
Underwater dance, just you and me!

Mermaids winked from coral lands,
Swam with jellybeans in our hands.
The current pulls a prank so sly,
Riding bubbles, we kiss the sky!

With each twist, a quirky turn,
Life's a pool, we laugh and learn.
Floating on our inflatable dreams,
Together we create the memes!

Journeys Through the Blue

Hop on a wave, we're on the go,
Riding the tides, moving like a pro.
Fish wear hats, it's quite the sight,
Giggling octopuses swim with delight!

In our goggles, we see it all,
Whales throwing parties, big and small.
Surfboards dance, the sea's our stage,
Crab conga lines, oh what a craze!

Seahorses twirl in a wavy race,
Splashing confetti, an ocean embrace.
With every wave, a story unfolds,
Sandy footprints, adventure bold!

So plunge into blues, feel the delight,
Where laughter echoes, and fish take flight.
Cheeky dolphins leap and flow,
In this watery world, we steal the show!

Ocean's Embrace

In sync we swirl like seaweed greens,
Chasing bubbles, we make funny scenes.
Surfing waves that tickle our toes,
The ocean giggles as our fun grows!

Crabs in sunglasses play peek-a-boo,
Our splashy dance, the ocean's debut.
The currents swirl like a dance hall floor,
Inviting us in, oh, we want more!

Floating around on a slice of pie,
Sipping seaweed shakes, oh my, oh my!
Toot sweet seagulls bring snacks galore,
We munch as the waves come crashing ashore!

Caught in the net of quirky dreams,
Where swimming feels like riotous schemes.
With every stroke, our laughter is heard,
In the embrace of waves, we're utterly stirred!

Fluid Horizons

As we plunge into watery glee,
Fish wear sunglasses, just wait and see!
With fins and flippers, we glide and roll,
Through skies of blue, we'll reach our goal!

The waves weave stories, funny and bright,
As dolphins twirl, they light up the night.
Laughing sea turtles join in the fun,
What a surreal race, we're on the run!

Underwater chases, bubbles a-fly,
Making a splash while the sea creatures sigh.
Tangled in kelp, we're all in a knot,
With laughter echoing, it's a real jackpot!

Our journey's a whirl, a giggling spree,
In this fluid world, come dance with me.
With every wave, our spirits feel light,
Let's ride the tide till the stars shine bright!

Confluence of Thoughts

In a river of ideas, I trip and fall,
Splashing wisdom on the wall.
Fish often giggle at my face,
As I swim in this mental race.

Bubbles rise with every gaffe,
Making the brook laugh, what a laugh!
My thoughts swirl like leaves on a breeze,
Yet here I am, trying to tease.

The current pulls me with a grin,
Who knew pondering could be such a sin?
Chasing ducks in a paper boat,
While all around, the wise folks gloat.

Oh, to float on a wave of jest,
While Einstein's ghost puts me to the test.
I'll paddle on with a wink and a jest,
In this current of nonsense, I'm truly blessed.

Sinking into Serenity

I sat in stillness like a log,
But then a frog asked, "Where's your jog?"
I smiled back, lost in my thoughts,
While he leapt high, as if he fought.

Every ripple tickled my chin,
A fish swam by, 'Are you in a spin?'
I pondered life between sips of tea,
As jokes from my mind danced wild and free.

The sun beamed down a golden beam,
I waved at clouds, lost in a dream.
A butterfly laughed, 'Join the fun!'
But I found joy just being a pun.

Serenity's great, but laughter's the best,
When nature joins in, we laugh with zest.
Oh, let's float where the giggles abound,
Sinking in joy where smiles are found.

The Flowing Path

On a path made of bubbling grins,
I stumbled once, where fun begins.
A turtle hollered, 'Slow your chase!'
But I was racing, oh, what a pace!

The pebbles danced beneath my feet,
As fish flipped out—what a treat!
I waved at reeds that shimmied sly,
While squirrels chuckled and fluttered by.

The current pulled with a teasing sigh,
'Catch me if you can!' it seemed to cry.
I replied with splashes, laughter galore,
And soon, all nature joined in the score.

Oh, the flowing path of playful cheer,
Where every turn brings a tickling leer.
Adventure awaits with every stroke,
As I laugh with the earth and share each joke.

Whispers of the Deep

Down below, where secrets sleep,
A snail asked if I wanted to leap.
I shrugged and floated, seeing the jest,
While jellyfish giggled, 'Just give it a rest!'

The whispers wrapped around my ear,
'Take off your shoes, come join us here!'
I splashed in circles, creating a ruckus,
While octopuses joined, saying, 'That's ludicrous!'

An eel swayed and told silly tales,
Of underwater cows and their mooing gales.
I chuckled at fish in a dance so weird,
As bubbles erupted, my laughter steered.

So deep in the sea, where humor reigns,
With every stroke, joy pours through my veins.
In the whispers of blue, I find my delight,
Laughing with critters, all day and all night.

The Calm of the Current

In my boat, I took a nap,
Dreams of fish with hats and cap.
Rivers giggled, streams replied,
Bubbles danced, the water sighed.

A raccoon swam with style and flair,
He wore my sunglasses—what a pair!
Otters rolling, making a fuss,
My snacks were gone, what's the fuss?

Waves like puppies licked my toes,
Chasing ducks dressed in pink clothes.
With every splash, I burst a laugh,
Oh, what fun, this silly bath!

I thought I'd fish but lost my bait,
Lured by laughter—it's just fate.
Floating here, I'll let it go,
Next time I'll be the star of the show!

Thalassic Whispers

Whispers from the ocean bright,
Jellyfish wiggling in sheer delight.
A crab danced with mad precision,
Clawing at my lunch, what a collision!

Seagulls caw, they aim for fries,
Eating like kings, oh how they rise.
Surfboards crashing, laughs abound,
Sharks swim by, they come to clown!

Rafting quests, we drift and glide,
While clam shells sing, we take a ride.
Fish with wigs swim past my face,
Who knew the sea could have such grace?

With every splash, I hear a cheer,
The tide gives hugs, they bring good cheer.
In this wet world of joy and fun,
Under the sun, we all are one!

Ebb and Flow

Riding waves like toddlers do,
Splashing water in shades of blue.
Snorkeling with some friendly clown,
A sockfish flipped, oh what a gown!

I fell off the float with quite a splash,
The dolphins laughed, oh what a crash!
With every swell, I gain some grace,
Just add the bubbles; they'll leave a trace.

Octopi juggling, what a sight,
They tossed my snacks, it was a fright!
Fish in sunglasses—what a spree,
Who knew the ocean loved to party?

The shore said, "Hey, we see you there!"
I waved back, my laugh in the air.
Ebb and flow, it's all pure bliss,
When the tide pulls back, I won't miss!

Weightless Wander

Floating freely like a kite,
Where gravity gives up the fight.
A sea cucumber waved hello,
Said, "Join the fun, just let it go!"

Bubbles tickled my silly feet,
Splat against my snack—a funny treat.
A walrus snorted, what a sound,
With every trip, we tumbled round.

Coral castles, bright and grand,
Unicorns swim—ain't life just bland?
Wobbly jelly tied my shoe,
Next time I'm taking a crew!

So on this ride, I'll lose all care,
With fishy friends, I'll wear my flair.
Weightless wander, what a thrill,
In this wacky world, there's time to chill!

Embracing the Current

I jumped in with glee, what a sight,
My friends giggled hard, what a fright!
Flippers flapping, I spin like a toy,
Chasing bubbles, oh what a joy!

The river laughed, it splashed my face,
I wrestled a fish, it took off in haste!
Water's my dance floor, I'm not alone,
With each slip and wiggle, I'm in the zone!

I paddled upstream, oh what a game,
Only to find I'm heading the same!
Laughing and splashing, we all do the wave,
Underwater shenanigans, we're so brave!

As I floated down, the turtles did grin,
I told them my jokes, they took it on chin!
So here I go, with a splash and a cheer,
Life's much better when you swim without fear!

Under the Skin of Water

Belly flops echo, a splash like a breeze,
My friends roll with laughter, it's all done with ease.
The fish stare amazed, they wonder aloud,
What kind of monster just joined the crowd!

I twirl like a star, in this shimmering sea,
Swirls of my chaos that surely can't be!
But here comes a wave, oh dear what a mess,
Spitting out giggles, what a slippery fest!

Noodles and rubber ducks roam all around,
In this wet wonderland, laughter's the sound.
I wear my goggles, my nose plugged tight,
Submerged in the silliness, what pure delight!

Then I try to swim, but I slip, what a sight!
Flapping about, like a bird in mid-flight.
With each cheerful flop, I discover anew,
That life's funniest moments are born in the blue!

Beneath the Surface

Bubbles arise where the giggles are found,
I splash like a seal, joyfully unbound.
The fish watch me dance, a comedic routine,
As I twist and I turn, like I've lost all my steam!

With a belly full of laughter, I swim without grace,
A conga line forms, we all know this space.
Duck diving down, finding treasures in sand,
When I pop back up, it's just so unplanned!

A crab pinches me hard, oh what a surprise!
I laugh at its pinch and roll up to the skies.
Floating so freely, each splish is a score,
What fun is this dance? It's never a bore!

From the depths of the lake, to the wide-open sea,
Water brings joy, it's just you and me.
So grab your floaties, and let's make a splash,
In this wacky adventure, we'll have quite the bash!

The Flow's Embrace

I zipped through the rapids, a wild ride ahead,
With laughter and squeals, I forgot all dread.
The river is waltzing, swaying with ease,
I tumble and tumble, rolling like leaves!

A fish tickled me, oh the cheeky little thing,
I puffed out my cheeks, no time for a fling!
Fins flapping wildly, I tried to keep pace,
But laughter erupts with each silly face!

Taking the plunge, I did it with flair,
My friends all went silent, and gasped in despair.
The splash was a symphony, my own kind of song,
Every ripple and giggle, we all sang along!

So here's to the fun, where the currents conspire,
Cascading in joy, like a live wire!
We dance with the tide, all worries erased,
In the flow's bright embrace, we are happily braced!

Flowing with the Stream

A fish forgot its direction, it's true,
Tangled in seaweed, feeling quite blue.
It wiggled and jiggled, oh what a sight,
Claiming it's dancing, with all of its might.

A turtle shouted, "Slow down, my friend!"
The fish just shrugged, it won't even bend.
"Life's more fun when you swim with glee!"
"And when you get lost, just follow me!"

They spun in circles, laughter like waves,
They'd both tell the tale, how fun life behaves.
With a splash and a flip, they roused the crew,
Who knew being lost could be so much fun too!

So here's to the flippers and fins, oh what a scream,
Every climb to the surface begins with a dream.
We'll float on the bubbles, and twirl in the blue,
When you cast aside worry, the current's for you!

Currents of Change

A river decided to change its course,
To ditch the banks and find a new source.
"I'm tired of boring!" shouted the stream,
"I'll roll over rocks and chase every dream!"

Along came a brook with a giggle and sway,
"Let's splash through the meadows, come out and play!"
They laughed as they tumbled, oh what a sight,
Splashing all creatures with smiles, what a bite!

The wise old fish said with a grin,
"You can change a path, but you won't win.
For rocks are relentless, and mud sticks too tight,
But hey, what's an adventure without a small fight?"

With bubbles of laughter, they zigged and they zagged,
Proving that change can be really quite tagged.
In the dance of the waters, with joy so immense,
Let's flow with the chaos, it makes perfect sense!

Deep Waters Await

In deep waters danced a clam with a crown,
"I'm royalty here, so don't bring me down!"
The octopus waved with eight arms a-spread,
"I'll paint you a picture!" — and turned it instead.

A crab scuttled by, with his pinchers held tight,
"What's all this fuss, in the depths of the night?"
"I'm the king of the rocks!" was the clam's great claim,
The octopus chuckled, "Who even knows your name?"

The turtle just shrugged, with a slow, steady pace,
"Friends, let's just enjoy this curious place.
With bubbles and laughter, we're all in this show,
Don't mind the drama—just go with the flow!"

So in deep waters, whimsy took flight,
With a pinch of silliness, oh what a delight!
With bubbles and crowns, it's the aquatic ballet,
Where shadows are dance partners, and fun leads the way!

Cascading Dreams

A waterfall giggled, cascading down loud,
"I'm the happiest dancer! Come join the crowd!"
The rocks provided rhythm, they clapped and they cheered,
While fish formed a chorus, for music was seared.

"Splash me a story!" called out a brave trout,
"I'll weave you a tale with no hint of doubt!"
With ripples and bubbles, they spun like a ball,
To the cadence of water, they danced one and all.

The nimble little frogs jumped to the beat,
"More leaps and more bounds—oh, life is so sweet!"
While the dragonflies twirled, with shimmer in flight,
The cascade of dreams continued through night.

So let's celebrate water, with joy and a splash,
In moments of fun, let the laughter just thrash.
With dreams in our hearts, we'll never run dry,
In cascading joy, we simply can't lie!

Flowing Towards Tomorrow

In a river of socks, I swim with glee,
Each pair a treasure, where could they be?
Floating on dreams, I paddle away,
Laughing at laundry that calls out to play.

With ducks as my crew, we sail through the mess,
Navigating bubbles, it's anyone's guess.
Why fight the chaos? Just join in the fun,
Splashing and quacking beneath the bright sun.

I surf on the waves of cereal tide,
Wheaties and Cheerios, oh, what a ride!
Who knew breakfast could have such a flair?
Giggles and grins float up in the air.

So come take a dip in this whirlpool of cheer,
With humor as lifejacket, there's nothing to fear!
We'll paddle and tease till the day turns to night,
In the flow of tomorrow, everything's right.

Whirlpools of Thought

In a whirlpool of ideas, I take my chance,
Spinning 'round theories like a wild dance.
Thoughts jumping like fish in a wiggly way,
Catch one and giggle, toss boredom away!

Paddling through nonsense, I float on a whim,
With humor as bait, my prospects are brim.
How does a potato learn to take flight?
We'll find out one day, or maybe tonight!

In this current of laughter, we trade all our woes,
Bubble-bursting jokes and silliness flows.
Tangled in laughter, we twirl like a reel,
The best of all catchphrases, it's goofy appeal!

As thoughts whirl and whirl, like a storm in the brain,
I'll grasp at the giggles, it's never in vain.
Out of the chaos, bright ideas will bloom,
In the whirlpools of thought, there's always room.

Submerged Serendipity

Deeper I plunge, in a pool full of quirks,
Each splash a new treasure, delightful perks.
Bubbles of fortune float up from below,
What kooky surprise will the deep waters show?

I swim with a dolphin who tells silly jokes,
Tickling my sides as he leaps and he pokes.
In this underwater circus, we frolic with glee,
The jellyfish dance, oh, so whimsically!

When fish start to sing, it's the best kind of tune,
I tap dance on reefs under a bright, laughing moon.
With octopus friends and a crab who can rhyme,
Life's never been better in this watery clime.

With a wave of my fin, I chase joy through the sea,
To find all the giggles that were left just for me.
Serendipitous moments, surface to share,
In a splash of silliness, there's magic in air.

Turning Tides

The tide rolls in with a grin wide and bright,
It carries my thoughts on its swell through the night.
Turning and twisting like a merry-go-round,
In a sea full of laughter, joy knows no bound.

Sandcastles crumble, but spirits are high,
With seagulls as jesters, they laugh in the sky.
A flip-flop floats by, on a quest of its own,
Chasing after sunlight, never alone.

Oh, surfboards of silliness parade on the waves,
Riding the laughter, the memory saves.
With each ebb and flow, there's a chuckle to find,
Humor's a treasure you can't leave behind.

So let's raise a toast to the tides that we ride,
To the funny little moments that never subside.
In the rhythm of water, with giggles that glide,
We're thriving forever on this playful tide.

Currents of the Heart

In love we swim, what a messy splash,
Tangled in waves, hoping for a dash.
Flipping our fins, like we know the score,
Trying to flirt, but we wash up ashore.

With giggles and grins, we float on by,
As seagulls squawk, we chuckle and sigh.
A heart's a buoy, bobbing at sea,
Caught in a whirlpool, oh, woe is me!

Each tick of the clock, like a tide it turns,
We wade through the laughter, the lesson we learn.
In this silly ocean, we fish for a smile,
And hope that the seaweed won't hold us awhile.

So come take the plunge, don't be shy,
With water-wings on, we'll aim for the sky.
In the surf of our dreams, let's make quite a stir,
For the currents of hearts can be quite the blur.

Rippled Reflections

Mirrors of water, we giggle and play,
With splashes like laughter, we swim through the day.
Look at my reflection, is that fish really me?
Or a soggy old sock, floating haplessly free?

Cannonballs echo in rippling delight,
As friends all around me take flight in their plight.
But who needs a plan when you've got a cool float,
A banana or llama, that's what we wrote!

The sun's on our backs, and the food's on the grill,
We race for the snacks, through the water we thrill.
Fins flapping wild, with a splash-back of glee,
In these rippling moments, oh, happy are we!

Look at the shadows dancing in glee,
A choreographed chaos, like squirrels on a spree.
With all of our shenanigans weaving our song,
In these ripples of joy, we continue along.

Uncharted Waters

Paddling through blues of unknown delight,
With oars made of laughter, oh, what a sight!
Is that a whale, or just my floating hat?
With giggles galore, we're not scared of that.

We frolic like dolphins, with no map in hand,
Searching for treasure in the wavy sand.
What's that in the distance? A dancing sea cow?
Oh just a mirage, but hey, we're here now!

Plotting our course with a compass of fun,
In waters uncharted, we'll outshine the sun.
With friends as our crew, we'll sail far and wide,
No need for directions, we'll just enjoy the ride.

So let's tip our hats to the waves, oh so grand,
With jellyfish jiggles and mermaid bandstands.
In uncharted waters, there's nothing to fear,
Just laughter and friendship, echoing clear.

Embracing the Abyss

Plunge deep below, where the silly fish joke,
With seaweed tickling, we dive till we croak.
Fins flapping wildly, we tumble in glee,
In this wacky abyss, it's just you and me!

What's that in the dark? A ticklish old eel?
Laughing and wriggling, what a comical deal!
With bubbles as giggles, we float side by side,
In the embrace of the depths, we joyfully glide.

Gazing at corals, all swirly and bright,
We twirl like the sea stars in playful moonlight.
Caught in a whirlpool of whimsy and cheer,
The abyss is our playground, so let's persevere!

So here's to the dive, to the dark and the strange,
Where laughter swims freely, and nothing can change.
In the belly of laughter, we find our own bliss,
Embracing the abyss with a clownfishy kiss!

Entwined with the Flow

Wrestling with a rubber duck,
I find my home's a bubbling muck.
In circles round, I spin and glide,
With laughter bubbling, waves my ride.

The goldfish stare as I pretend,
To race the tide like a best friend.
My neighbor's cat, it gives a shout,
As I splash water all about.

The hose's spray becomes my sea,
I'm Captain Splash, oh can't you see?
A snorkel made from a garden hose,
In this wild world, my fun just grows.

The pool's my ocean, couch my boat,
With jellyfish made from bubble coats.
In my own world of silly dreams,
I surf the chaos and silly streams.

A Leap into the Deep

With goggles on and flippers tight,
I plot my launch mid-midsummer light.
A cannonball—oh, what a sight!
I belly flop, my splashes bright.

My friends all cheer, it's quite a show,
While I float by like a big ole mango.
I wriggle like a fish out of luck,
Crashing waves, just hoping not to duck.

Waves chuckle softly at my plight,
As I flail and thrash with all my might.
A seagull laughs; it's quite the scene,
In this wild world, I'm the queen!

Every splash, a watery giggle,
The sun goes down, but I still wiggle.
Who knew that water could spark such fun?
In my goofy dance, the day's not done!

Bowing to the Waves

I tip my hat to the rolling tide,
Respectfully bow, then jump inside.
The waves they giggle, tickle my toes,
As I splash back, oh how it flows!

Each misstep's met with playful tease,
I practice my moves like a cork on the breeze.
A graceful turtle? I wish I were,
But I'm more like a clumsy, flopping blur.

The seashells whisper, "You want to play?"
I nod my head, then slip and sway.
With friends around in a bubble-ache,
We'll ride these waves for fun's own sake.

The ocean's dance is wild and free,
In this madcap whirl, I just can't flee.
So here I am with a goofy pose,
As waves come laughing, I lose my clothes!

The Pulse Beneath

Beneath the surface, secrets swirl,
With quirky fish that leap and twirl.
I try to swim with style and grace,
But often end up in a soppy race.

The currents twist like a dance so bold,
A hilarious twist, or so I'm told.
My snorkel's stuck, what a grave error,
Yet still I laugh with bubbling terror.

The seaweed tugs at my goofy hair,
As I waddle out, a finless bear.
My friends all wave, but they can't believe,
How many times I'll take a dive and leave.

But in this pulse of liquid fun,
I find my joy, I'll not be shunned.
With fits of laughter, waves I flout,
In this lively sea, there's never doubt!

The Glistening Depth

Bubbles rise and giggles flow,
Flopping fish put on a show.
Swimmers slip, a splashy sight,
Underneath, the world feels light.

Rubber ducks with silly grins,
Paddle faster, let the fun begin!
Whirlpools whirl, it's all a race,
Splash on friends, it's water's pace.

Goggles tight, a clownfish dance,
Wiggling fins in a funny trance.
Laughs echo from sea to shore,
What a splash, we all want more!

So grab a float, don't slip away,
Make waves, we're here to play!
In the depths where giggles swim,
Life's a joke — let's dive in!

Shifting Waters

Water here, then water there,
Jump and splash without a care.
Float like clouds, oh what a tease,
Watch out for the squirt gun breeze!

To the left, then to the right,
Somebody's floundered, what a sight!
Rubber mallets, splash my shoe,
Now I've got a soggy view!

Swirls of colors, what a mess,
Noodle fights lead to duress.
Slippery rocks, a perfect trap,
I just tripped — what a funny flap!

In the waves, let laughter reign,
Jokes will echo, no one is sane.
Let's swim around and laugh out loud,
Join me now, let's draw a crowd!

A Liquid Dreamscape

In a sea of jello, what a treat,
Frogskin boots make summer sweet.
Floating pies, what a sight,
Jump in quick, it's quite a bite!

Dancing turtles twirl and dive,
In this goo, we all come alive.
Pickled fish with silly hats,
Join the fun, grab your cats!

Giggling waves, they tease and pout,
Squirty squids, who could live without?
Jellybeans drift, oh what a flow,
In this splash, we steal the show!

Sloshing round in our dreamscape,
Clumsy kicks, but who could escape?
Under the water's jovial gleam,
Life's a game, or so it seems!

Below the Flowing Surface

Wiggle your toes in the flowing blue,
What's that bubbling? Oh, it's you!
Under waves, laughter spins,
Swirling whirlpools pull us in.

Fishy faces swim with glee,
Let's make silly fishy tea!
Goggles gleam with a wacky glare,
Shallow dives send bits of hair.

Belly flops and splattery grins,
Jumping high — let the chaos begin!
Under the antics, magic plays,
Snorkeling dreams fill our days.

So come along for the fishy ride,
Laughs and waves, it's a wild tide!
Life below, a silly lure,
Bubbles bursting — that's for sure!

A Journey Through Waters

Flip-flops fly, we race to the bay,
In a splashy contest, we forget the way.
Goggles on tight, we look like a clown,
As mermaids giggle and fish swim around.

With every misstep, we tumble and roll,
Our laughter echoes—it's out of control.
A sardine smiles as we pass him by,
"Why not join in?" he seems to imply.

Buckets of water, our heads now look wet,
We paddle like penguins, no sign of regret.
Each wave a surprise, we dance and we sway,
A watery jig on this bright, sunny day.

At the end of this romp, with seaweed in hair,
We strike silly poses for memories to share.
For who needs a map when you're lost in delight,
In the salty embrace of this sun-drenched fight?

The Undercurrent's Call

Under the surface, a ticklish brigade,
With fishy companions, we make our parade.
Bubbles like giggles escape from our lips,
While turtles look on, sharing seaweed chips.

We flap and we flop, what's the right way to float?
Should we paddle, or soar like a bright little boat?
A crab waves his claw, looks fancy and spry,
"Don't take life too seriously!" we wail with a cry.

The shark's in a rush, he's late for a show,
"Catch you later, folks!" and off he does go.
We chase after seahorses that wobble about,
In this underwater circus, we laugh and we shout.

As the sun kisses water, we're caught in its glow,
Our skills are unique—well, you know how they go.
With a splash and a snicker, we make quite the scene,
In this watery world, we reign as the queens!

Waves of Discovery

Riding the roller, what a goofy ride,
On waves that giggle, we surf with pride.
Our floats like donuts, they bob and they sway,
As seagulls join in—hey, come out to play!

The squirt of a whale sends us all in a spin,
We pop back up, with wide, toothy grins.
A dolphin does flips, oh what a show,
We cheer him on loud, but he steals the flow!

Round and round, our beach ball takes flight,
A seastar shouts, "That's not quite polite!"
Caught in the chaos, we giggle and shriek,
With each twist and turn, it's laughter we seek.

Finding treasures like shells with a twist,
In this ocean of wonders, it's hard to resist.
With splashy hijinks and silly little slides,
We're riding the tides, where the fun never hides!

Echoes Beneath the Waves

Dancing with fish, call it a jolly good time,
With wiggles and spins, we create our own rhyme.
"Look at me!" a blowfish puffs out his chest,
We all start to giggle, it's simply the best.

Bubbles like laughter float up to the sky,
As we twirl and we spin, not a single one dry.
A shrimp grasps the mic and starts to croon,
"Join in the fun!" he sings to the moon.

Tangled in seaweed, we laugh till we cry,
In this underwater escapade, time just flies by.
A crab with a hat struts by like a pro,
"Life's a beach party!" he says, putting on a show!

As we rise to the surface, all giggles and cheer,
With salty sea smiles, everything's clear.
Echoes of laughter bounce high on the tide,
For the joy of the ocean is ours to abide.

Navigating the Unknown

Splashing about with a grin,
Lost in a world of aquatic spin.
Flippers flapping, oh what a sight,
Who knew it'd be this much delight?

Maps are useless in a pool,
Chasing fish—now that's my rule!
Round and round I swirl and twirl,
A fishy dance, oh what a whirl!

I bumped a turtle, it gave me a stare,
Did it just judge my hair?
With bubbles rising, I shout and cheer,
Who knew being wet could bring such a tear?

Sailing through chaos, a glorious mess,
Laughter bubbles, I must confess.
The thrill of splashes, let's have some fun,
Navigating joy, we've only begun!

Echoes Beneath

Under the waves, what do I hear?
A guppy chorus, quite sincere!
In bubbles and giggles, I find my cue,
The ocean's laughter, always brand new.

With each splash, the fishy cheer,
"Swim faster, kid, the coast is near!"
I swirl my tail and chime along,
Fin-tastic echoes, I can't go wrong!

A crab snaps back, "Hey, watch the show!"
"Don't pinch my fins, just let it flow!"
Laughter ripples as I glide with grace,
Dancing through water, I find my place!

The sea's my stage, what fun to scheme,
Every splash and giggle builds my dream.
Echoes of joy in every dive,
In this wavy world, I feel alive!

Currents of the Heart

In a bubble bath, I feel the flow,
Tangled in suds, I steal the show.
With rubber ducks as my loyal crew,
We conquer the foam—yup, that's what we do!

A tidal wave of giggles arise,
As I splash-wrestle a soap-sud surprise.
Bubbles pop like a joyful spark,
Sailing on laughter, we light up the dark!

I call to the sponge, "Join my quest!"
It floats away—guess it needed a rest.
Drifting on currents of pure delight,
I sail through the night, my heart feels light!

Wet and wild, I live my dream,
Finding joy in the drippy stream.
Currents of laughter, my heart sets sail,
Bubbling with joy, I shall prevail!

The Dance of Ripples

Waves and wiggles, what a fine dance,
Spinning in circles, I take a chance.
A splash here, a twirl there, laughter galore,
Can't stop my jig, oh, give me more!

The fish join in, and oh, what a sight!
They shimmy and shake, "Get ready for flight!"
With every ripple, we groove and sway,
Making the most of this watery play!

A seahorse twirls, "Let's change the beat!"
I trip on a fin, then back on my feet.
Laughing at kelp as it swings left and right,
Caught in this whirl, oh, what pure delight!

With a final splash, we finish the show,
The dance of the ripples, moving just so.
In a world of giggles, I'll make my mark,
As I glide through the waves, dancing 'til dark!

Embracing the Undertow

In the water, we twirl and spin,
Finding joy, where chaos begins.
With a splash, we lose our way,
Yet laughter's the game we play.

Flippers flying, aimless strife,
Oops! Did I just swallow life?
Gulping bubbles, what a taste,
Water sport's a fun-filled waste!

From the side, they cheer and scream,
"Just aim for the edge, it's a dream!"
But here I am, flailing about,
A fish out of water, without a doubt.

In the whirl, I find my friend,
Holding tight, we'll never bend.
With crazy spins, we blast away,
The ocean's our stage, come what may!

Riding the Waves

Surfboards flying, what a sight,
Wipeout moments steal the light.
Each tumble's a giggle, oh what fun,
Even the seagulls start to run!

The ocean shouts, "Catch me if you can!"
I'm busy planking like a beached man.
Every rise a glorious feat,
Then, whoops! I'm scattering feet.

Hoopla echoes, laughter spills,
Kites crashing, oh, what thrills!
Friends around with waves to ride,
We're ocean-bound, let's joke and glide!

With sandy toes and salty hair,
Challenge the tide, if you dare!
Every crest's a rollercoaster,
Life's a splash, just be a roaster!

The Depths We Explore

Let's plunge into the sea so blue,
The fish parade, just me and you.
Goggles fogged, I can't see clear,
But what's this? A bubble, dear?

Neon fish, the ocean's feast,
I'm just a clumsy, giggling beast.
In the coral, hide and seek,
Chasing krill, it's quite unique!

Every swirl, a tangled dance,
Watch me try and take my chance.
Finding treasures, oh what fun,
Oops! That's a shoe, not a gun!

Bubbles form, a comedy show,
Watch me stumble, and there I go!
Twisting, spinning, what a thrill,
Deep-sea antics give me a chill.

Submersion in Possibility

Water sloshes, laughter rings,
Thoughts take flight on fishy wings.
With a splash, I take the lead,
Who knew that waves could make you bleed?

Underneath, a treasure waits,
In the depths, swim towards fates.
Twinkling dreams in sandy trails,
Look out, world! Here comes the gales!

Bubbles dance, a wavy line,
The sea's a riot, it's feeling fine.
Arching through like nimble seals,
Each glide reveals what joy feels.

With whimsy wrapped in salty air,
Every plunge shows that we dare.
In the depths of possibility,
Life's a splash, a pure agility!

www.ingramcontent.com/pod-product-compliance
Lightning Source LLC
Chambersburg PA
CBHW062110280426
43661CB00086B/442